HOORAY FOR PILOTS!

by Elle Parkes

BUMBA BOOKS™

LERNER PUBLICATIONS ◆ MINNEAPOLIS

Note to Educators:

Throughout this book, you'll find critical thinking questions. These can be used to engage young readers in thinking critically about the topic and in using the text and photos to do so.

Lerner Publications Company
A division of Lerner Publishing Group, Inc.
241 First Avenue North
Minneapolis, MN 55401 USA

For reading levels and more information, look up this title at www.lernerbooks.com.

Library of Congress Cataloging-in-Publication Data

Names: Parkes, Elle, author.
Title: Hooray for pilots! / by Elle Parkes.
Description: Minneapolis : Lerner Publications, 2016. | Series: Bumba books—Hooray for community helpers! |
    Audience: K to Grade 3. | Includes bibliographical references and index.
Identifiers: LCCN 2016001054 (print) | LCCN 2016014949 (ebook) | ISBN 9781512414424 (lb : alk. paper) |
    ISBN 9781512414752 (pb : alk. paper) | ISBN 9781512414769 (eb pdf)
Subjects: LCSH: Air pilots—Juvenile literature.
Classification: LCC HD8039.A4 P37 2016 (print) | LCC HD8039.A4 (ebook) | DDC 629.132/52—dc23

LC record available at https://lccn.loc.gov/2016001054

Manufactured in the United States of America
1 – VP – 7/15/16

Expand learning beyond the printed book. Download free, complementary educational resources for this book from our website, www.lernerresource.com.

Table of Contents

Pilots

Pilots fly airplanes.

They fly people to different places.

Pilots sit in the cockpit.

There are many buttons

and screens.

Screens show pilots where

to fly.

Most pilots fly with a copilot.

The copilot and pilot work together.

They both control the airplane.

Why do you think pilots need copilots?

Pilots check the weather before flying.

They fly a different path if there is bad weather.

Why might bad weather make it hard to fly?

11

Pilots use a radio.

They talk to other pilots.

Pilots talk to workers at the

airports too.

They find out where to land.

Pilots wear a uniform.

They wear a hat and a jacket.

Some have a badge with wings.

Why do you think pilots wear a uniform?

Pilots have to learn how
to fly.

They take exams and

flying lessons.

They practice flying for

many hours.

Some pilots work

long hours.

They fly many airplanes

each week.

Pilots make sure airplane trips

are safe.

They help people see the world!

Pilot Tools

cockpit

uniform

badge

screen

buttons

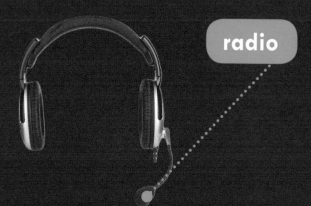

radio

22

Picture Glossary

badge

a small object pinned on clothes to show who someone is

cockpit

the control area in the front of the airplane

copilot

the person who helps the pilot

uniform

a special set of clothes worn for work

Index

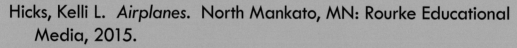

Read More

Hicks, Kelli L. *Airplanes*. North Mankato, MN: Rourke Educational Media, 2015.

Minden, Cecilia. *Pilots*. Mankato, MN: The Child's World, 2014.

West, David. *Planes*. Mankato, MN: Smart Apple Media, 2015.

Photo Credits